X

D1483251

AMERICAN JUSTICE

Seven
Famous
Trials of
the 20th
Century

L. L. Owens

Perfection Learning®

Cover Design: Michelle Glass
Inside Layout: Michelle Glass

Image Credits: Corbis/Electric chair p. 18; Corbis/Civil Rights march p. 30; Corbis/Sharon Tate and Roman Polanski p. 33; Corbis/Manson family members p. 35; Corbis/Manson w/police p. 38; Corbis/O.J. Simpson's verdict reading p. 50; Associated Press/O.J. Simpson, Nicole w/their children p. 45; Associated Press/Ron Goldman p. 45; Standard Oil of New Jersey Collection— Photographic Archives, University of Louisville/Segregated drinking fountain p. 28

Art Today: Inside Cover and pp. 6, 7, 8, 9, 12, 13, 15, 16, 20, 21, 22, 24 Albert Einstein, 27, 32, 36, 41(bottom), 42; Library of Congress/Dwight D. Eisenhower p. 24; Art Today: Justice Scale on pp. 10, 11, 13, 15, 17, 19, 21, 23, 24, 30, 34, 35, 37, 39, 42, 47, 51; Art Today: file folder and gavel on pp. 5, 12, 20, 26, 31, 40, 44; Department of Defense p. 41 (top); Clipper/Constitution p. 43

About the Author

Lisa L. Owens grew up in the Midwest. She studied English and journalism at the University of Iowa. She is a full-time editor and freelance writer.

Other books by Ms. Owens include *The Spirit of the Wild West, Eye on Ancient Egypt*, and *Bigfoot: The Legend Lives On*. Ms. Owens lives near Seattle with her husband, Timothy Johnson.

Note

This book contains information about well-known trials and notorious crimes. Please be aware that, as a result, many serious and upsetting criminal actions are discussed.

TABLE OF CONTENTS

Introduction 4

Chapter 1. Leopold and Loeb Lose the "GAME" . . 5

Chapter 2. The Lindbergh Baby Kidnapping 12

Chapter 3. Spies Among Us:
Julius and Ethel Rosenberg 20

Chapter 4. A Step Forward:
Brown v. Board of Education 26

Chapter 5. Charles Manson's "Family" Business . . 31

Chapter 6. *The New York Times*
Wins the Right to Publish 40

Chapter 7. O. J. Simpson Stands Trial for Murder . . 44

Glossary 53

Index 56

LeRoy Collins
Leon County Public Library
200 W. Park Avenue
Tallahassee, FL 32301

INTRODUCTION

*Kidnapping. Murder. Spying. School **segregation**. Freedom of the press.*

The most-watched American trials of the 20th century were focused around these issues. Several of these well-known trials are discussed in this book.

They became famous because we found them so interesting. The issues addressed our deepest beliefs. And they touched on our deepest fears.

You'll read about the following real-life characters and cases that captivated the world.

- two young college students who killed a boy as an intellectual game
- the kidnapping and murder of an American hero's baby boy
- a couple sentenced to death for betraying their country
- an African American man who fought for his daughter to receive the same educational opportunities given to white children
- a madman who talked others into killing for him
- the U.S. government's attempt to limit a newspaper's right to publish sensitive information
- a wealthy sports hero accused of the cold-blooded murders of his ex-wife and her friend

Each of these cases left its mark on the 20th century.

Leopold and Loeb Lose the "GAME"

Case at a glance

Year: 1924
Trial Location: Chicago, Illinois
Defendants: Nathan Leopold Jr. and Richard Loeb
Criminal Charges: Kidnapping and murder
Kidnapping and Murder Victim: Bobby Franks
Verdict: Guilty
Sentences: Life imprisonment plus 99 years for each **defendant**

Murder: For the Thrill of It

It was 1924. Richard Loeb and Nathan Leopold committed murder. They were bored. So they did it for the thrill. They wanted to prove that they could.

Loeb was in graduate school at the University of Chicago. He was just 18. The murder had been his idea.

He had always been obsessed with crime. So he wanted to commit the "perfect" one.

Leopold, 19, was already in law school at Chicago. He was devoted to his friend Loeb. He was eager to help him with anything—*even murder.*

Their plan was cold and heartless.

1. Kidnap a boy from a wealthy family.
2. Knock him out.

3. Take him to a **culvert** near the Pennsylvania Railroad tracks.
4. **Strangle** him.
5. Throw away his clothes and other personal items.
6. Stuff the body in the culvert.
7. Walk away. Never look back. And never get caught.

The men thought their plan was brilliant.

On May 21, 1924, they rented a car. They drove to the Harvard Preparatory School. It was time to commit the crime. And they were looking for a victim.

Soon they saw Loeb's 14-year-old cousin, Bobby Franks. They knew that Franks came from a wealthy family just as they did.

Leopold pulled up next to the boy. Franks gladly accepted a ride. Within minutes, he was dead. He suffered several blows to the head. (Loeb hit him with a chisel.)

Leopold and Loeb followed their plan. They got rid of Franks' clothes. They poured acid over his body. And they hid the **corpse** in the culvert. They were sure that it would never be found.

Next they went out to dinner. They acted as if nothing had happened!

Later, they washed Franks' blood out of the car. And they typed and sent a note to his father. They asked for $10,000.

The next morning, some workmen noticed Franks' foot. It was sticking out from the culvert. They also found Leopold's custom-made eyeglasses. Leopold and Loeb had not been as careful as they thought.

The police found Leopold's typewriter in the Jackson Park Harbor. They also traced the glasses to him.

At first, Leopold lied. He said that he'd dropped his glasses while bird-watching. But that story fell apart.

The police questioned the young men for an entire day. Both denied having any involvement in the murder.

On the second day, Loeb confessed. He thought that Leopold had "**snitched**" on him. But he hadn't.

Soon Leopold confessed too. Each of the men claimed that the other had actually killed Franks.

The Public Watches

Americans could not get enough news about this crime. The media played up the most fascinating angles. For example, the young men had high levels of intelligence. There was no "real" **motive** for the killing. And both men had families of wealth and social position.

7

The families hired Clarence Darrow as a **defense** attorney. He was the most famous criminal attorney of the **era**.

Darrow's skill had saved about 50 murderers from 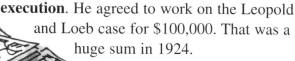 **execution**. He agreed to work on the Leopold and Loeb case for $100,000. That was a huge sum in 1924.

The trial began on July 23, 1924. The public seemed to want the accused murderers to hang. In fact, they expected it. People across the land were angered that two rich kids viewed murder as a sport. They couldn't believe that the boys had thought it would be something fun to do.

Darrow knew what he faced. He changed Leopold and Loeb's pleas from "not guilty" to "guilty." It was a surprising move.

This turned the trial into a hearing. There would be no jury, just a judge. The judge would decide whether the defendants would be executed or serve life in prison.

Darrow's hope was to persuade the judge that his clients should live. He said

> We want to state frankly here that no one believes these defendants should be released. We believe they should be permanently **isolated** from society.

Darrow showed that his clients lived in a **fantasy** world. They had no grasp of **reality**. He argued that society could benefit from studying their minds.

At one point, Darrow asked the court

> Why did they kill little Bobby Franks? They
> killed him as they might a spider or a fly. For the
> experience. They killed him because they were
> made that way. Because somewhere . . .
> something slipped. That happened. And it calls
> not for hate. But for kindness. For charity. For
> consideration.

Toward the end of his **summation**, Darrow pleaded for the men's lives. He said

> You may hang these boys by the neck until
> they are dead. But you will turn your face toward
> the past. I am pleading for the future. For a time
> when hatred and cruelty will not control the
> hearts of men. When we can learn by reason
> and judgment and understanding and faith that
> all life is worth saving. And that mercy is the
> highest [trait] of a man.

9

Darrow's speech was powerful. When he finished, the courtroom was silent. Tears streamed down the judge's cheeks.

Two days later, the judge announced his **verdict**. Leopold and Loeb were each sentenced to life in prison for murder. They each received an additional 99 years for kidnapping.

Life After the Trial

Leopold and Loeb were sent to the Joliet prison. They were allowed to work together on several prison projects.

Loeb was killed in 1936. Another inmate slashed him with a razor. He died the next day.

Leopold would miss his friend for the rest of his life. He became a model prisoner. He used his time to
- learn 27 foreign languages
- design a new prison education system
- teach in the prison school
- reorganize the prison library
- work as an X-ray technician in the prison's hospital
- volunteer to receive an experimental malaria vaccine

Leopold's Thoughts on Remorse

Looking back . . . I cannot understand how my mind worked then. For I can recall no feeling then of **remorse**. Remorse did not come until later. Much later.

It did not begin to develop until I had been in prison for several years. It did not reach its full flood for perhaps ten years.

Since then, for the past quarter century, remorse has been my constant companion. It is never out of my mind.

Sometimes it overwhelms me completely. To the extent that I cannot think of anything else.

—from Nathan Leopold's book *Life Plus 99 Years*

Leopold's Thoughts on Punishment

I've spent 32 years here. Is that sufficient punishment for what I did?

I don't know the answer to that. Because I don't know how to measure punishment. . . .

I've forfeited every chance for happiness. I've forfeited a chance for a family. Whether this is sufficient, I don't know.

—from Nathan Leopold's book *Life Plus 99 Years*

In 1958, the parole board released Leopold from prison. He had been jailed for 34 years.

He moved to Puerto Rico. He hoped to live out the rest of his life in peace. He earned a master's degree. He wrote books, including *The Birds of Puerto Rico*. He taught math. And he worked in church missions and hospitals.

Leopold died of a heart attack in 1971.

Hollywood Looks at the Case

To date, there are three movies based on the Leopold and Loeb case.

- *Rope* in 1948
- *Compulsion* in 1959
- *Swoon* in 1992

Note: All three films were made for adult audiences.

11

THE LINDBERGH BABY KIDNAPPING

Case at a glance

Year: 1935
Trial Location: Flemington, New Jersey
Defendant: Bruno Richard Hauptmann
Criminal Charge: Murder
Murder Victim: Charles A. Lindbergh Jr.
Verdict: Guilty
Sentence: Death by electrocution

On March 1, 1932, Charles and Anne Morrow Lindbergh's baby was kidnapped. He was taken from his crib in the family's Hopewell, New Jersey, home.

The world watched as the couple tried to get him back. The public mourned when he was found dead. And they rejoiced when Bruno Richard Hauptmann was convicted of the murder.

12

Kidnapping Rings

In the early 1930s, there were organized kidnapping rings. They had sprung up in every major U.S. city.

The criminals in these rings stole children. Then they demanded money from suffering parents. That money was called ransom. It was asked for in exchange for the child.

The wealthy were popular targets. And the Lindberghs were wealthy.

Sadly, these crimes still occur.

The Night of the Kidnapping

The baby's name was Charles A. Lindbergh Jr. He was 20 months old.

Anne put him to bed that night. He had a cold. So she made sure he was warm and comfortable.

Anne left his side at 7:30 p.m.

The nursemaid was Betty Gow. She was still in the nursery when Anne left. She tidied up. She made sure the baby was covered. Then she opened a French window halfway.

Betty checked a short time later. The baby was fast asleep.

The Lindberghs had dinner at about 8:30.

At 10:00, Betty entered the nursery. It was time for another routine check. She shut the window and turned on the heater.

Then she turned toward the crib. It was empty!

She quickly found Anne. She asked, "Do you have the baby, Mrs. Lindbergh?"

Anne did not.

"Perhaps Colonel Lindbergh has him then," said Betty.

The women searched the house. Charles didn't have the baby. None of the other servants had the baby. He was gone.

Charles examined the baby's room. The window was unlatched. It was open just a crack. A white envelope rested on the sill.

Charles didn't touch it. He knew it was a ransom note. And it was evidence.

He called the police at 10:25. Within 20 minutes, state law enforcement agencies had been notified. By 11:00, the investigation was well under way.

Clues at the Scene

The police found four main pieces of evidence.
1. The ransom note
2. An abandoned homemade ladder
3. A shoe print in the mud near the ladder
4. A chisel near the ladder

A rung on the ladder was broken. Police thought it had likely broken as the kidnapper came back down the ladder. So the kidnapper—with the baby—had probably fallen about five feet to the ground.

The kidnapper clearly knew the layout of the house. And that person knew the schedule of the household. Police felt that more than one person had helped plan the crime.

The Ransom Note

The handwriting on the note was awkward. Experts thought the writer was probably Scandinavian. Or perhaps the writer was German. They decided this because of the placement of the dollar signs. Also, the spellings used showed that the writer didn't know English that well.

Here is the exact text of the ransom note.

Dear Sir!

Have 50.000$ redy 25.000$ in 20$ bills 15.000$ in 10$ bills and 10000$ in 5$ bills.

After 2–4 days we will inform you were to deliver the Mony.

We warn you for making anyding public or for notify the Police

the child is in gut care. Indication for all letters are singnature and 3 holes.

Charles A. Lindbergh: An American Hero (1902–1974)

Charles Lindbergh was a well-known pilot. His nickname was "Lucky Lindy."

On May 21, 1927, he landed his plane outside Paris. He'd completed the first successful nonstop solo flight over the Atlantic Ocean. The nation went wild. He became a hero.

Lindbergh married Anne Morrow in 1929.

After their son's death, the Lindberghs moved to

England. They wanted to escape publicity. The couple stayed there for a few years.

In 1953, Lindbergh won a Pulitzer Prize. It was for his book *The Spirit of St. Louis*.

In 1954, he was made brigadier general in the Air Force Reserve.

A Nightmare Becomes Reality

The Lindberghs were heartsick. Anne wrote letters to help her think through the situation. Charles tried to control the investigation. But both were helpless.

The public followed news of the case for the next several weeks. The Lindberghs received many fake ransom notes. Floods of mail from well-wishers also arrived.

Soon a meeting with the kidnapper was set up. A **go-between** delivered $50,000 to the supposed kidnapper.

In exchange, Charles received instructions. They told him where to find the baby. But the baby wasn't there.

On May 12, the couple's worst nightmare came true. The baby was found dead. He had been left in the woods just a few miles from home.

It appeared that he had died from a blow to the head. Police felt that he had been dead since the night he was taken. He may have even died in the fall from the ladder.

It was two years before an arrest was made.

16

Hauptmann Caught with Ransom Money

Bruno Richard Hauptmann was a carpenter. And he was a German **immigrant**. He had entered the country illegally.

In September 1934, Hauptmann bought gas. He paid with a $10 gold certificate. This was an unusual way to pay.

The federal government first issued gold certificates in 1863. The paper currency notes were printed with orange ink. They were backed by 100% reserves of gold coin. They could be cashed in on demand. General use ended in 1933.

The gas station attendant noted Hauptmann's license number. And he took the certificate to the bank.

The bill was identified as part of the Lindbergh ransom money. Hauptmann was soon arrested.

Police found more ransom money in his garage. They also found the phone number of the Lindberghs' go-between. It was written on the wall in a closet.

The Trial

The trial was a major media event. The public watched with great interest. Everyone wanted justice for "Lucky Lindy," his beautiful wife, and their slain child.

Things went badly for Hauptmann. There was much **circumstantial evidence** against him.

- He possessed some of the ransom money.
- Handwriting experts testified that he had written the ransom notes.
- The ladder was traced to him.

No witnesses placed Hauptmann at the scene of the crime. The footprint wasn't proven to be his. And his fingerprints were not found in the baby's room. They were not on the ransom notes either.

Still, he was found guilty. He was electrocuted April 3, 1936. The public felt that justice had been served.

As recently as 1992, Hauptmann's widow tried to clear his name. She believed her husband was framed. And his conviction should be overturned.

Some experts agree with Mrs. Hauptmann. They say that the case was mishandled. And it should be reopened.

So far, the courts have been unwilling to take another look.

One thing seems clear, though. The Lindbergh baby case will be discussed well into the 21st century.

The Lindbergh baby kidnapping trial is often referred to as the "trial of the century."

On February 2, 1999, the *Today* show ran a segment about the 20th century's most famous trials. They had taken a survey to see what viewers thought.

There were 3,857 respondents. These are the results.

Question: What do you think is the "trial of the century"?

Responses:

24%—The 1995 Trial of O. J. Simpson

21%—The 1946 Nazi War Crimes Trial

20%—The 1999 Clinton Impeachment Trial

14%—The 1925 Scopes "Monkey" Trial

7%—The 1935 Lindbergh Baby Kidnapping Trial

4%—The 1970 Trial of Charles Manson

3%—The 1951 Trial of Ethel and Julius Rosenberg

2%—The 1992 and 1993 Los Angeles Police Officers' "Rodney King Beating" Trial

1%—The 1921 Sacco and Vanzetti Trial

1%—The 1924 Trial of Nathan Leopold and Richard Loeb

1%—The 1931-1937 Scottsboro Trials

1%—The 1954 and 1966 Trials of Sam Sheppard

1%—The 1969 "Chicago Seven" Trial

0%—The 1906 Trial of Harry Thaw

0%—The 1907 Trial of "Big Bill" Haywood

0%—The 1921 Trial of "Fatty" Arbuckle

Source: MSNBC.com

Note: Percentages may not total to 100% due to non-responses.

Chapter 3

Spies Among US:
Julius and Ethel
ROSENBERG

Case at a glance

Year: 1951
Trial Location: New York, New York
Defendants: Julius Rosenberg, Ethel Rosenberg
Criminal Charges: Plans, or conspiracy, to commit wartime **espionage**
Verdict: Guilty
Sentences: Death by electrocution for both Rosenbergs

Julius and Ethel Rosenberg lived in New York City. Julius was an engineer. He worked for the U.S. Army Signal Corps.

He was very involved in politics. For a time, he and Ethel belonged to the **Communist Party**. Their political views matched those held by many people in the Soviet Union.

They quit the party in 1943. But Julius agreed to become part of a Soviet spy ring. He gave U.S. atomic bomb secrets to the Soviets.

The Federal Bureau of Investigation (FBI)

The FBI was established in 1908. It is part of the U.S. Department of Justice.

The agency investigates certain **violations** of federal laws. The issues they deal with can include

- espionage
- bank robbery
- **sabotage**
- kidnapping
- **extortion**
- fraud
- assault or killing of the president of the United States
- transporting of stolen property across state lines

Arrests

The FBI gathered evidence against Julius. They arrested him at home July 17, 1950. They did not arrest Ethel.

Witnesses reported that Ethel had been present during conversations about the espionage. But there was not enough evidence to prove she was part of the spy ring.

Soon, though, the FBI arrested Ethel anyway.

J. Edgar Hoover was director of the FBI. It was his idea to try to build a case against Ethel. He hoped that Julius would confess to protect his wife.

Julius's confession would be valuable. The FBI hoped he would name others in the spy ring.

Hoover said

> If Julius Rosenberg would furnish details of his
> extensive espionage activities, it would be
> possible to proceed against other individuals . . .
> proceeding against his wife might serve as a lever
> in this matter.

Ethel was arrested August 11, 1950. Julius heard the news.
But he did not confess.

The Rosenbergs Stand Trial

The Rosenberg trial began on March 6, 1951. Morton
Sobell was also a defendant at this trial. But public attention
was focused on the Rosenbergs.

The trial attracted international attention.

Irving Saypol was a United States attorney. He represented
the government in this case. In his opening remarks, he said
that the defendants had committed a capital
crime. He said it was "the most serious
crime which can be committed against the
people of this country."

The jury was told that the Rosenbergs
gave Soviets information about the atomic
bomb. That could lead to danger. Perhaps
it would mean the destruction of the U.S.

There were many witnesses for the
prosecution. The only defense
witnesses were the Rosenbergs
themselves.

Excerpt of Julius Rosenberg's Testimony

Emanuel H. Bloch was one of the Rosenbergs' attorneys. He asked the witness many questions. A few include

Emanuel H. Bloch: Do you believe in the overthrow of government by force and violence?

Julius Rosenberg: I do not.

E. H. Bloch: Do you believe in anybody committing acts of espionage against his own country?

Julius Rosenberg: I do not believe that.

The Court: Well, did you ever belong to any group that discussed the system of Russia?

Julius Rosenberg: Well, Your Honor, if you are referring to political groups—is that what you are referring to?

The Court: Any group.

Julius Rosenberg: Well, Your Honor, I feel at this time that I refuse to answer a question that might tend to **incriminate** me.

Witness David Greenglass was Ethel's brother. While in the army, he had worked in the Manhattan Project. This is where the U.S. developed the atomic bomb. David admitted to leaking information to Julius.

David painted a detailed picture of Julius's spy efforts. He claimed that Julius had

- paid David for information about the atomic bomb
- held secret meetings with other spies
- planned to escape to the Soviet Union
- burned evidence
- used a Jell-O box, cut in two, as a signal to another spy

Julius Rosenberg denied all these accusations.

23

Chapter

A Step Forward:
Brown v. Board of Education

Case at a glance

Year: 1954

Trial Location: Washington, D.C.

Appellants: Oliver Brown and several other parents of African American children

Defendant: Board of Education of Topeka, Kansas

Claim: That school segregation violated African American students' 14th-Amendment rights

Decision: Segregated schools violate the equal protection clause of the 14th Amendment.

A Little Girl Is Turned Away from School

In September 1950, Linda Brown was about to start third grade. She lived with her family in Topeka, Kansas.

Schools in Topeka were segregated. Linda, a black child, was not allowed to attend the school for white children.

To get to school, Linda had to leave home early in the morning. She had to walk alone through a busy **switchyard**. Then she had to wait for a bus. The school was about one mile from home.

The all-white school was nearer the Browns' home. It was a safer seven-block walk.

So Oliver Brown decided to enroll Linda there. Oliver was Linda's dad.

After all, Brown reasoned, it would be much easier for Linda to get to school. Safer too. And why should young Linda have to go to all that trouble? The fact that she was black—that her skin simply was "not white"—seemed a ridiculous reason.

The school principal promptly turned away the Browns. He would not allow Linda to enroll.

The NAACP Gets Involved

Brown went to see McKinley Burnett. Burnett was head of Topeka's branch of the National Association for the Advancement of Colored People (NAACP).

The NAACP decided to help Brown file a lawsuit. It was time to fight for an end to segregation in public schools.

During that era, segregation was common in Kansas and elsewhere. And it was not just in schools. Segregated bathrooms, hotels, theaters, and restaurants were standard.

The lawsuit, however, would address only the public schools. The lawyers argued that black children were being unfairly denied educational opportunities that white children received.

They also said that simply improving all-black schools was a poor solution. Black children would still suffer by being educated separately from their white peers.

The U.S. District Court for the District of Kansas ruled. They decided that segregation would continue.

The case was appealed. It went straight to the U.S. Supreme Court. That court heard it twice.

The decision was announced on May 17, 1954. Chief Justice Earl Warren said

> We conclude that in the field of public education, the **doctrine** of "separate but equal" has no place. Separate educational facilities are **inherently** unequal.

This ended legal segregation in public schools.

The Court's Opinion

Warren wrote the court's **opinion**. It explained how the court reached its decision.

In this case, all nine justices agreed. Part of the opinion read

> In approaching this problem, we cannot turn the clock back to 1868 when the Amendment was adopted. . . . We must consider public education in light of its full development and its present place in American life.

The court had concluded that "segregation deprived members of the minority race of equal opportunities."

They said that segregation "generates a feeling of **inferiority** . . . that may affect . . . hearts and minds in a way unlikely to be undone."

In other words, children denied equal educational opportunities might have a more difficult time as adults. They might lack the motivation—or even the knowledge—to succeed. And this was clearly unfair.

Hugo L. Black
Harold H. Burton
Tom C. Clark
William O. Douglas
Felix Frankfurter
Robert H. Jackson
Sherman Minton
Stanley Reed
Earl Warren

A Struggle

Although the Supreme Court had ruled, change was slow.
In 1955, the court said that *all* American schools should end segregation. And that they should do so "with all **deliberate**

speed."

During the civil rights movement of the 1960s, all forms of segregation were banned. But it still took 20 years of "deliberate speed" to desegregate the nation's schools.

Oliver Brown didn't live to see that. But he would have been proud. Because he helped make it happen.

Chapter 5

CHARLES MANSON'S "Family" Business

Case at a glance

Years: 1970–1971

Trial Location: Los Angeles, California

Defendants: Charles Manson, Susan Atkins, Patricia Krenwinkel, Leslie Van Houten

Criminal Charges: First-degree murder and conspiracy to commit murder

Murder Victims: Sharon Tate, Jay Sebring, Abigail Folger, Voyteck Frykowski, Steven Parent, Leno LaBianca, Rosemary LaBianca

Verdict: Guilty

Sentences: Death for all defendants; later changed to life in prison

Manson's Troubled Childhood

Charles Manson was born in 1934. Birth records list his name as "No Name Maddox." His childhood was filled with hardship.

Manson never knew his father. He took the name "Manson" from one of his mother's husbands.

Manson sometimes lived with his mother in broken-down hotels. Often, though, he lived with other relatives. His mom was in jail for a while. She had been convicted of armed robbery.

When Manson was 12, he ran away. Soon he was stealing from stores. He was caught. And he was sent to live at Father Flanagan's Boys Town.

Four days later, he stole a car and drove away. An arrest for armed robbery followed when he was 13.

Manson as an Adult

It is clear that Manson suffered as a child. As he grew up, he learned to make others suffer. He also learned how to control others' actions.

Manson admired Adolf Hitler. Hitler was a German **dictator**. His **racist** beliefs and thirst for power led to the

Adolf Hitler

Holocaust during World War II.

Manson was quoted as saying that Hitler was a "tuned-in guy." Not surprisingly, Manson was also a racist who yearned for power.

In the 1960s, he started his own small society, or *commune.* The members of the commune lived at Spahn Ranch. They looked up to Manson.

In fact, they feared and worshipped him. (Just as Hitler's followers had feared and worshipped *him.*)

They believed everything he said. And they did everything he asked them to do. Manson's followers were known as the "Family."

Manson took advantage of his followers' trust. Through them, he was able to create a drug and crime ring.

Manson was 35 at the time of the trial. He had already spent half his life in juvenile detention centers and jails.

His long criminal record included convictions for

- rape
- burglary
- grand theft auto
- assault
- forgery
- mail theft
- attempted escape
- parole violations

A psychiatrist said that he was "emotionally unstable," "assaultive," and "dangerous."

Manson has bragged about murdering more than 35 people. He has been married and divorced twice. And he has two known children.

The Tate-LaBianca Murders
August 9, 1969

A young actress named Sharon Tate was murdered at her home. So were her three houseguests and a friend of the groundskeeper.

Tate was pregnant with her first child. Her husband was director Roman Polanski. He was out of town. So Tate entertained some friends to keep her mind off missing him.

Outside, four young people gathered. They were members of the Family. They were there on Manson's orders. And they prepared to invade the home.

Family Members at the Tate-Polanski House

Susan Atkins
Linda Kasabian
Patricia Krenwinkel
Charles "Tex" Watson

Watson cut the phone lines. Two others climbed over the fence.

Eighteen-year-old Steven Parent was in his car. He had just visited his friend the groundskeeper.

Watson shot him to death on sight. Then he ordered Kasabian to guard the Family car.

Meanwhile, the other Family members murdered Tate and her friends.

It was a bloody scene. The killers brutally stabbed their victims. Then they left a message on the front door.

They used the victims' blood. They wrote "PIGS."

August 10, 1969

Manson drove his Family to the LaBianca home. He parked and took Watson into the house with him.

The two men returned to the others. Manson told them that he had tied up the two people inside.

Kasabian said later that she thought Manson said, "Don't let them know you are going to kill them."

Manson drove off, leaving the others to slay the LaBiancas.

The scene was similar to the night before. Police found the LaBiancas stabbed to death in their home.

Blood was smeared on their walls too. The grim messages included "**DEATH TO PIGS**" and "**HELTER SKELTER.**"

Family Members at the LaBianca House

Charles Manson
Linda Kasabian
Patricia Krenwinkel
Leslie Van Houten
Charles "Tex" Watson

left to right: Leslie Van Houten, Susan Atkins, and Patricia Krenwinkel

The Trial

This trial was one of the longest and most expensive in California history. It was highly publicized worldwide.

The judge had to issue a *gag order.* That forbids witnesses and lawyers from talking to the media about the trial. They particularly can't give any information that is not part of the evidence.

The first day of **testimony** was July 24, 1970. Manson entered the courtroom. All eyes turned to him. He had carved an *X* into his forehead.

Atkins, Krenwinkel, and Van Houten noticed the *X.* Soon they, too, had carved *X*s into their foreheads. This **cult** leader still held power over his followers.

Manson asked to represent himself at trial. The judge swiftly denied that request.

Manson seemed to view the trial as a game. His comments at trial were strange and unpredictable. He often shouted during others' testimony. In a rage once, he even lunged at and threatened the judge.

Here are excerpts from Manson's own testimony.

The Court: *Do you have anything to say?*

Charles Manson: Yes, I do.

. . . I never went to school. So I never growed up in the respect to learn to read and write so good. So I have stayed in jail. And I have stayed stupid. I have stayed a child while I have watched your world grow up. And then I look at the things that you do. And I don't understand.

. . . I don't think like you people. You people put importance on your lives.

Well, my life has never been important to anyone. Not even in the understanding of the way you fear the things that you fear. And the things you do.

I know that the only person I can judge is me.

If you put me in [jail], that means nothing. Because you kicked me out of the last one. I didn't ask to get released. I liked it in there. Because I like myself.

I like being with myself.

. . . These children that come at you with knives, they are your children. You taught them. I didn't teach them. I just tried to help them stand up.

Most of the people at the ranch that you call the Family were just people that you did not want. People that were alongside the road. That their parents had kicked them out. Or they did not want to go to Juvenile Hall. So I did the best I could. And I took them up on my garbage dump.

And I told them this that in love there is no wrong.

. . . It is not my responsibility. It is your responsibility. It is the responsibility you have towards your own children who you are neglecting. And then you want to put the blame on me again and again and again.

. . . If I could get angry at you, I would try to kill every one of you. If that's guilt, I accept it.

. . . That is not my responsibility. I don't tell people what to do.

One of the prosecution's biggest challenges would be to convict Manson. He had not physically committed the murders. But he had planned them. And he had ordered the Family to carry out those plans.

On January 25, 1971, the jury reached its verdict. Manson and the other defendants were found guilty. All were sentenced to death on March 29, 1971. They were to die in the gas chamber.

None of them were executed, however. In February 1972, California banned the death penalty.

Manson and the others are all serving life sentences.

The Two Family Members Who Weren't Tried with the Rest

Linda Kasabian

Kasabian acted as a lookout during the killings. But she did not personally kill anyone.

She testified against Manson and the others. She did so in exchange for immunity. That meant she could not be prosecuted for the crimes.

Charles "Tex" Watson

Watson participated in the murders. He later fled to his parents' home in Texas. He was arrested there.

Watson's lawyer got him a separate trial. He was found guilty and sentenced to death. His sentence was later changed to life in prison.

Will Manson Ever Go Free?

On March 27, 1997, Manson had his ninth parole hearing. It lasted about one hour. Manson said

> I do a lot of underworld things. I've been in the underworld all my life. Since I was a child. You make a mistake and cross me, I'll get you. It's that simple. Sooner or later.

The parole board discussed their decision for just 20 minutes. Then they announced that Manson would not receive parole. In other words, he would not be set free.

The board said that Manson "would pose an unreasonable risk and danger to society." They said he would be "a threat to public safety if released from prison."

Manson replied, "I accept this decision. That's cool."

Charles Manson's next parole hearing is scheduled for 2002.

Chapter

The New York Times
Wins the Right to Publish

Case at a glance

Year: 1971
Trial Location: Washington, D.C.
Appellant: The United States
Defendant: The New York Times Company
Claim: That, in the interest of national security, the government had the right to prevent *The New York Times* from publishing the Pentagon Papers
Decision: The government could not prevent *The New York Times* from publishing the Pentagon Papers.

"Top Secret"

In 1971, the U.S. was involved in the Vietnam War. Many citizens were against that involvement.

That spring, Daniel Ellsberg and Anthony Russo Jr. stole two reports. The studies had been prepared by the U.S. Department of Defense.

One was the "History of U.S. Decision-Making Process on Vietnam Policy." The other was the "Command and Control Study of the Gulf of Tonkin Incident."

Both documents dealt with U.S. involvement in Vietnam. Both were classified as "TOP SECRET." The public was *not* supposed to see them.

The men **leaked** the documents to *The New York Times* and *The Washington Post.*

On June 13, the *Times* ran its first article about the documents. These documents were now known as the "Pentagon Papers."

The government went to the U.S. District Court for the Southern District of New York. They asked the court to stop the *Times* from publishing additional articles about the Pentagon Papers.

The government claimed these papers contained sensitive information. They said printing them would be a national security risk.

The court required the *Times* to stop publication of the series until the case was heard.

The *Washington Post* Enters the Fray

The *Post* published excerpts from the Pentagon Papers on June 18, 1971. The government took similar action against that newspaper. But the case against the *Times* was the government's focus.

A Swift Decision

Two weeks later, the case had made its way to the U.S. Supreme Court. The question before the court was

> Can the government block publication of controversial information before the public even sees it?

On June 30, the court ruled that it could not.

The Constitution of the United States

This case was about 1st-Amendment rights. The 1st Amendment is part of the Constitution. The Constitution is the official statement of the U.S. system of government.

The document was written in 1787 and passed, or ratified, in 1788. It took effect in 1789.

The ideas upon which the document is based are

- limited government
- responsible government
- federalism

The document begins with a short introduction, or preamble. Seven articles follow. They address the powers and procedures of government.

- organization
- powers and procedures of the legislative branch (Congress)
- powers of the president and executive branch
- powers of the judiciary branch, including the Supreme Court
- states' rights
- procedures for adjusting, or *amending*, the Constitution

Twenty-six amendments follow the articles. The first ten are known as the Bill of Rights. Here is the text of the 1st Amendment.

> Congress shall make no law respecting an establishment of religion, or prohibiting the free exercise thereof; or abridging the freedom of speech, or of the press; or the right of the people peaceably to assemble, and to petition the Government for a redress of grievances.

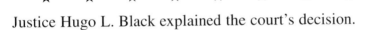

Justice Hugo L. Black explained the court's decision.

James Madison and the other Framers of the 1st Amendment . . . wrote in language they . . . believed could never be misunderstood:

"Congress shall make no law . . . abridging the freedom . . . of the press . . ."

Both the history and language of the 1st Amendment support the view that the press must be left free to publish news. Whatever the source. Without censorship, **injunctions**, or prior restraints. . . .

The decision upheld the 1st-Amendment right to freedom of the press. And that decision stands today.

O. J. SIMPSON

STANDS TRIAL FOR MURDER

┌─────────────── Case at a glance ───────────────┐

Year: 1995
Trial Location: Los Angeles, California
Defendant: Orenthal James "O. J." Simpson
Criminal Charge: Murder
Murder Victims: Nicole Brown Simpson and Ronald L. Goldman
Verdict: Not guilty

Los Angeles

June 12, 1994

Nicole Brown Simpson, 35, was O. J. Simpson's ex-wife. She was murdered just outside her home. It happened sometime after 10 P.M. on June 12, 1994.

Ron Goldman, 25, was also killed that night. He had been returning a pair of sunglasses to Nicole. Her mom had left them behind at a restaurant. Ron was a waiter there.

The killer slashed Nicole's neck. Then he stabbed Ron at least 30 times.

Nicole and O. J.'s two young children were inside. The police later found them in an upstairs bedroom. They had slept through the whole thing.

At 12:10, Nicole's Akita led a passerby to the horrible scene. The dog was upset. Its feet, legs, and belly were soaked in blood.

Some people believed that there was more than one killer that night. Others thought the murder was drug-related. Some thought it was a case of mistaken identity.

A Suspect Emerges

O. J. Simpson, however, quickly became the prime suspect.

Police arrived at his home to tell him the news of Nicole's death. But Simpson was gone. He'd taken a midnight flight to Chicago.

The police questioned Brian "Kato" Kaelin. He lived in a guest house on Simpson's property.

Kaelin said that he'd heard loud thumps on his wall. He thought it happened at about 10:40.

Detective Mark Fuhrman went outside to check the area. He found a bloodstained glove. It matched a glove found near Ron's body at the murder scene.

Fuhrman and Detective Ronald Phillips also found drops of blood. They were on the driveway, the path to the front door, and the entryway to the house.

Soon the detectives announced that the property was a crime scene. They took Simpson's white Ford Bronco. It had blood in it too.

The police questioned Simpson the next day. By June 17, the police planned to arrest him. But they couldn't find him.

A. C. "Al" Cowlings knew where Simpson was. Cowlings was driving along an L.A. freeway in his own white Bronco. And Simpson was in the car.

The police were notified. It turned into an unusually slow "car chase."

TV news interrupted regular programming. About 95 million people watched the 90-minute chase.

They listened as Cowlings reported by cellular phone. He said that Simpson was **suicidal**. Simpson even held a pistol to his head.

Cowlings eventually drove back to Simpson's home. Simpson was arrested.

The media reported that Simpson had written a suicide note.

Police found the following in Cowlings' car.

- Simpson's passport
- $8,750 in cash and traveler's checks
- a loaded gun
- a false goatee and mustache
- a change of clothes
- photos of Simpson's two youngest children

On June 20, O. J. Simpson was charged with the double murders.

O. J.'s Note

This letter has been called Simpson's "suicide" letter. It was read at a press conference.

> To whom it may concern:
>
> First, everyone understand I have nothing to do with Nicole's murder. I loved her. Always have and always will. If we had a problem, it's because I loved her so much.
>
> Recently, we came to the understanding that for now we were not right for each other. At least for now. Despite our love, we were different. And that's why we . . . agreed to go our separate ways. . . .
>
> Like all long-term relationships, we had a few downs and ups. I took the heat New Year's 1989. Because that's what I was supposed to do. I did not plead no contest for any other reason but to protect our privacy. [I] was advised it would end the press hype.
>
> I don't want to belabor knocking the press. But I can't believe what is being said. Most of it is totally made up. I know you have a job to do. But as a last

wish, please, please, please, leave my children in peace. Their lives will be tough enough.

I want to send my love and thanks to all my friends . . .

Whatever the outcome, people will look and point. I can't take that. I can't subject my children to that. This way they can move on. And go on with their lives. Please. If I've done anything worthwhile in my life. Let my kids live in peace from you (press).

I've had a good life. I'm proud of how I lived. My mama taught me to do unto others. I treated people the way I wanted to be treated. I've always tried to be up and helpful. So why is this happening?

I'm sorry for the Goldman family. I know how much it hurts. Nicole and I had a good life together. All this press talk about a rocky relationship was no more than what every long-term relationship experiences. All her friends will confirm that I have been totally loving and understanding of what she's been going through.

At times I have felt like a battered husband . . . But I loved her, make that clear to everyone. And I would take whatever it took to make it work.

Don't feel sorry for me. I've had a great life, great friends. Please think of the real O. J. and not this lost person. Thanks for making my life special. I hope I helped yours.

Peace and love,
O. J.

Note: This letter was edited by the media to correct spelling errors.

"Absolutely, 100 Percent Not Guilty"

The trial began on July 22, 1994.

The judge asked Simpson, "How do you plead?"

Simpson replied, "Absolutely, 100 percent not guilty, Your Honor."

Another "Trial of the Century"

The trial lasted 21 months. A staggering amount of media attention was focused on it. It was the most watched and discussed trial in history.

Judge Lance Ito allowed cameras in the courtroom. Because it was televised, millions of people watched.

Some people were glued to their TV sets every day. People even missed work to see important testimony.

Others videotaped the trial. They watched only the parts that interested them.

Many felt that two trials were occurring. One was in the courtroom. And one was in the "court of public opinion."

People associated with the case became famous. Lawyers and witnesses showed up on news and talk shows. Many of them wrote books about the case.

Celebrities often popped up in the Simpson trial "audience." Everyone wanted to see this spectacle firsthand.

> "Children, children, thank you. That will be enough."
> —Judge Lance Ito, speaking to the bickering attorneys during a **sidebar**, March 6, 1995

Controversial issues were at the center of the case.

The defense said that Simpson had been framed. They said that a racist police force had planted evidence pointing to him.

Also, they showed that Fuhrman had expressed racist views in the past. And that he'd lied about his actions under oath.

Lying under oath is a crime. It's called *perjury*.

The prosecution showed Simpson's history of beating Nicole. This type of information is sometimes used to illustrate a pattern of behavior. It's a pattern that starts with random incidents of **domestic abuse**. The violence increases over time. The abuse can sometimes lead to murder.

DNA evidence was also a big part of the trial. The prosecution's experts talked about blood and hair samples found at the scene. They said that DNA tests proved they belonged to Simpson.

The defense countered by saying that DNA tests are flawed. They said if Simpson's hair and blood really were at the scene, the police had put them there.

It was a long, **grueling** trial.

On October 3, 1995, the jury announced its verdict— "Not guilty."

They had decided that Simpson's guilt had not been proven "beyond a reasonable doubt."

Some people were overjoyed at this outcome. Others were devastated.

Simpson vowed to help "find the real killers."

The Los Angeles Police Department and the district attorney had no leads on other suspects. They considered the case closed.

O. J. Simpson—Before and After the Trial

Simpson was a football hero. He had won the Heisman trophy. And he was a popular spokesperson, a sports commentator, and an actor.

He was a favorite American figure. He was wealthy. And he seemed to lead a good life. But that was before the murders.

Afterward, Simpson was jailed. He stood trial for the murders. His public image was changed forever.

After his **acquittal**, Simpson won custody of his two youngest children. Then the Goldmans and the Browns filed a **civil suit** against him.

The suit found him responsible, or liable, for the deaths of Nicole and Ron. He was ordered to pay $33.5 million in **damages**.

Simpson was forced to sell his home. A 1999 auction of his belongings raised $430,000. That money went toward the damages.

But as the Goldmans' lawyer Gary Caris said, the money barely "put a scratch" in Simpson's debt.

Trial by the Numbers

Interesting statistics from the Simpson trial include

Number of days Simpson spent in jail—474

Number of days jurors were **sequestered**—266

Length of closing arguments—4 days

Length of opening statements—4 days

Length of deliberations—less than 4 hours

Average age of juror—43

Number of jurors picked—12 plus 12 alternates

Number of jurors dismissed—10

Number of witnesses—defense 54; prosecution 72

Days of testimony—defense 34; prosecution 99

Exhibits presented during testimony—defense 369;
    prosecution 488

Number of motions filed—433

Number of attorneys who presented evidence in
    court—defense 11; prosecution 9

Number of times the judge "pulled the plug" on
    television—2

Cost—estimated $9 million for Los Angeles County

Amount earned by each of the 12 jurors and 2
    remaining alternates—$1,330

Length of official court transcript—more than
    50,000 pages

Number of media credentials issued—more than 1,000

Number of telephone lines installed in press room—250

Seating capacity in courtroom—80

Fines imposed on defense—$3,000

Fines imposed on prosecution—$850

Fines imposed on others—$1,800

Source: The Associated Press

GLOSSARY

appeal	legal action in which a case is taken to a higher court to review the lower court's decision
appellant	one who appeals a judicial decision
acquittal	having a not-guilty verdict given
circumstantial evidence	evidence that points to something being true because of circumstances surrounding it
civil suit	lawsuit about private rights (as opposed to criminal laws)
Communist Party	group who believes in a government that controls all business and industry
corpse	dead body
cult	small group of people devoted to a particular set of beliefs
culvert	drainage ditch or large drainage pipe
damages	monetary settlement decided upon by the court
defendant	person who is standing trial
defense	team that represents a defendant at trial; also, the set of arguments presented in favor of the defendant at trial
deliberate	careful, steady pace
dictator	ruler who has complete control

DNA	abbreviation of "deoxyribonucleic acid"—a person's genetic makeup
doctrine	belief; a rule
domestic abuse	abuse between spouses or in another family situation
era	period in time
espionage	act of spying
execution	death as a punishment for a crime
extortion	illegal demand for money or property
fantasy	make-believe
go-between	person who acts on behalf of one person and a third party
grueling	trying or taxing to the point of exhaustion
Holocaust	mass slaughter of Jews and others by the Nazis during World War II
hysteria	behavior showing uncontrollable fear
immigrant	person who moves to a new country to live permanently
incriminate	to give proof of misconduct
inferiority	sense of being lower in importance and value
inherent	by nature
injunction	court order that stops an action
isolate	to separate from others
leak	to make available
motive	reason
opinion	reason for court's decision

prosecution	team that brings a legal action against a defendant
racist	person who holds racial prejudices and believes in the false notion that a given race is superior to others
reality	state of being real
remorse	sense of guilt for past wrongs
sabotage	action meant to hinder a nation's war effort
segregation	deliberate separation or isolation of a race, class, or ethnic group
sequester	to isolate
sidebar	short conference between lawyers and the judge at trial
snitch	to inform
strangle	to choke to death by pressing on the throat
suicidal	in a state to take one's own life
summation	lawyer's final speech at trial in which the main arguments are reviewed
switchyard	switching facilities of a power station
testimony	evidence
verdict	final decision of a judge or jury in a trial
violation	breaking of a rule or policy

INDEX

Atkins, Susan, 31, 34, 35, 36
Bloch, Emanuel H., 23, 24
Board of Education of Topeka,
    Kansas, 26–30
Brown, Linda, 26–30
Brown, Oliver, 26–30
Burnett, McKinley, 28
Caris, Gary, 51
Cowlings, A. C. (Al), 46–47
Darrow, Clarence, 8–10
Ellsberg, Daniel, 40
espionage, 20–25, 54
Family, the, 31–36, 38, 39
Federal Bureau of Investigation, 21
1st Amendment, 42–43
Folger, Abigail, 31
14th Amendment, 26, 29
Franks, Bobby, 5, 6–7, 9
Frykowski, Voyteck, 31
Fuhrman, Mark, 46, 49
Goldman, Ronald L., 44–46, 51
Gow, Betty, 13–14
Greenglass, David, 23
Hauptmann, Bruno Richard, 12,
    17–18
Hitler, Adolf, 32
Hoover, J. Edgar, 21, 22
Ito, Lance, 49, 52
Kaelin, Brian (Kato), 46
Kasabian, Linda, 34, 35, 39
kidnapping, 4, 5, 6, 10, 12, 13, 19,
    21
Krenwinkel, Patricia, 31, 34, 35,
    36
LaBianca, Leno, 31, 34–35
LaBianca, Rosemary, 31, 34–35
Loeb, Richard, 5–11, 19

Leopold, Nathan Jr., 5–11, 19
Lindbergh, Anne Morrow, 12, 14,
    16, 17
Lindbergh, Charles A., 12, 13, 14,
    15–16, 17
Lindbergh, Charles A. Jr., 12–14,
    19
Manson, Charles, 19, 31–39
National Association for the
    Advancement of Colored
    People, 28
New York Times, The, 40–43
Parent, Steven, 31, 34
Phillips, Ronald, 46
Pentagon Papers, 40–42
Rosenberg, Ethel, 19, 20–25
Rosenberg, Julius, 19, 20–25
Russo, Anthony Jr., 40
Saypol, Irving, 22
Sebring, Jay, 31
segregation, 4, 26–30, 55
Simpson, Nicole Brown, 44–46,
    47–48, 50, 51
Simpson, Orenthal James (O. J.),
    19, 44–52
Sobell, Morton, 22, 24
Tate, Sharon, 31, 33, 34
U.S. Constitution, 26, 29, 42–43
U.S. Department of Defense, 40
U.S. District Court, 29, 41
U.S. Supreme Court, 29, 30, 42–43
Van Houten, Leslie, 31, 35, 36
Vietnam War, 40, 41
Warren, Earl, 29, 30
Washington Post, The, 41, 42
Watson, Charles (Tex), 34–35, 39